By Canoe & Moccasin

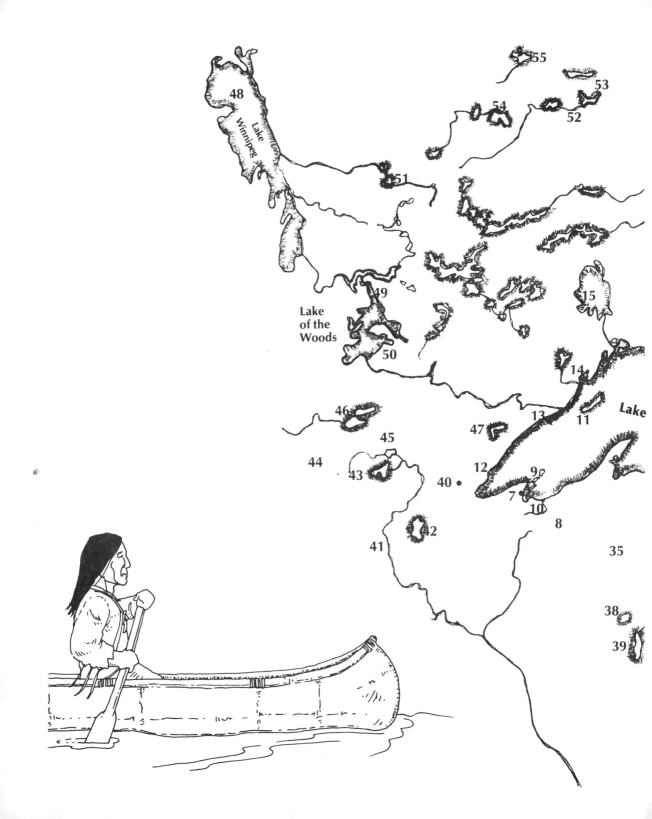

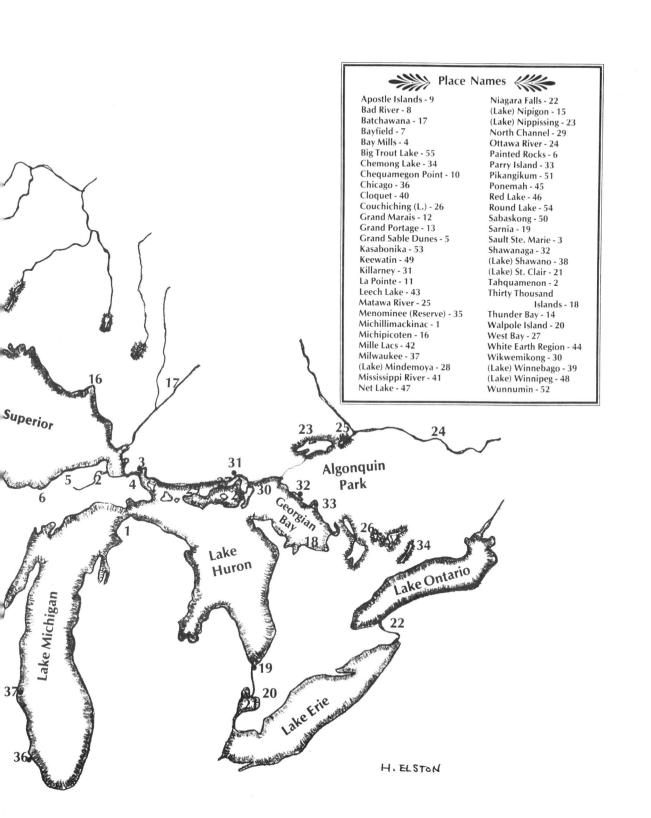

Place Names

Apostle Islands - 9
Bad River - 8
Batchawana - 17
Bayfield - 7
Bay Mills - 4
Big Trout Lake - 55
Chemong Lake - 34
Chequamegon Point - 10
Chicago - 36
Cloquet - 40
Couchiching (L.) - 26
Grand Marais - 12
Grand Portage - 13
Grand Sable Dunes - 5
Kasabonika - 53
Keewatin - 49
Killarney - 31
La Pointe - 11
Leech Lake - 43
Matawa River - 25
Menominee (Reserve) - 35
Michillimackinac - 1
Michipicoten - 16
Mille Lacs - 42
Milwaukee - 37
(Lake) Mindemoya - 28
Mississippi River - 41
Net Lake - 47

Niagara Falls - 22
(Lake) Nipigon - 15
(Lake) Nippissing - 23
North Channel - 29
Ottawa River - 24
Painted Rocks - 6
Parry Island - 33
Pikangikum - 51
Ponemah - 45
Red Lake - 46
Round Lake - 54
Sabaskong - 50
Sarnia - 19
Sault Ste. Marie - 3
Shawanaga - 32
(Lake) Shawano - 38
(Lake) St. Clair - 21
Tahquamenon - 2
Thirty Thousand
        Islands - 18
Thunder Bay - 14
Walpole Island - 20
West Bay - 27
White Earth Region - 44
Wikwemikong - 30
(Lake) Winnebago - 39
(Lake) Winnipeg - 48
Wunnumin - 52

H. ELSTON

By Canoe & Moccasin

Some Native Place Names
of the Great Lakes

by Basil H. Johnston

Illustrations by David Beyer

WAAPOONE
PUBLISHING & PROMOTION
Lakefield, Ont. K0L 2H0

Published by

WAAPOONE
PUBLISHING & PROMOTION
Lakefield, Ont. K0L 2H0

Third printing March, 1992

ISBN 0-9692185-1-6

Canadian Cataloguing in Publication Data

Johnston, Basil H, 1929 -
  By canoe and moccasin

ISBN 0-9692185-1-6

1. Ojibwa Indians - Legends - Juvenile literature. *
2. Indians of North America - Great Lakes Region -
Legends - Juvenile literature. 3. Legends - Great
Lakes Region - Juvenile literature. 4. Indians of
North America - Great Lakes Region - Names -
Juvenile literature.
E99.C6J65 1986   j398.2'08997   C86-094463-8

Design - Suzanne Wood
Printed by HOMESTEAD STUDIOS
Woodview, Ontario, Canada

Contents

Stories of His Travels

Preface

She was born in Mississauga, he in Oshawa; they married in Toronto, went to Niagara Falls for their honeymoon; they now work and live in Ottawa and take their vacations in Muskoka.

Such place names have become so changed through usage and pronunciation that few know that they are "American Indian" in origin. It is likely that fewer still know what the words mean or signify.

The person living in *Mississauga* may indeed know that "Indian" peoples once inhabited the area. They may not, however, realize that this word means "the large mouth or outlet of a river." It is derived through a fairly common Anishinaubae practice of naming a place after some unique or distinct characteristic within the area.

Oshawa means "to go to the other side" and suggests there was traffic of some kind conducted in that locality. Torontonians have come to accept "the place of meeting" as the meaning of *Toronto*. That may be, but it may also come from *Thorontohen*, an Iroquoian term meaning "timbers on the waters".

Niagara, today regarded as a place of romance and a wonderful starting point for wedded bliss, was no more than a "bisected bottomland" to the practical Tuscarora who called it *Onginaahra*.

Ottawa really means "to sell", not "to trade" as is generally assumed. But perhaps no objection should be made to this widely accepted meaning, because it describes the business conducted in the capital.

It is just as likely that the term *ottawa* or *odauwau* is a derivative of *odauwuhnshk,* a word referring to a kind of "bulrush" that grows in the river and which the people used in fashioning mats and doorway curtains. It is Anishinaubae practice to refer to the river as *odauwau-zeebi* for this profusion of bulrushes along parts of its course and to speak of the inhabitants as *odauwau-ininiwuk,* "men of the bulrushes."

To the old people, *Muskoka* evoked images of "a red land," either from the crimson of autumn leaves or from the ochre of the soil.

This story of the travels of Nanabush in pursuit of the enemies of his people will provide the meaning of common "Indian" names, regardless of border considerations. For there were no boundaries when this territory was occupied by the Anishinaubaeg.

Basil H. Johnston

PRONUNCIATION KEY

The Roman alphabet and system are not suitable for the Ojibway language. The a, b, c, characters or any combination thereof can show neither guttural nor nasal sounds, nor the halfway sounds between "d" and "t", "g" and "k", and "b" and "p". Another system needs to be developed in which the orthography is linked with the prefixes and suffixes.

Until someone devises such an orthographic system for the Ojibway language, a number of spelling systems must be endured. The Johnston variation follows.

There are two reasons why I chose to vary the orthography. One was to encourage enunciation; the other was to avoid confusion in the use of certain vowel sounds and to reserve certain consonants and combinations for specific purposes as dictated by prefixes, and notably the "tch"; "dj"; "ch" sounds.

The main points of departure from other spelling systems are:
"Au" to represent the "a" sound as in father.
"Ae" to represent an "a" for which there is no comparable sound in English.
"Ee" to represent the long "e" sound as in metre.
"I" has been retained to represent the short "i" as in pit.
"Zh" to represent the "zh" sound that frequently occurs.
"Hn" to represent and indicate a nasal sound.

In cases where the second consonant of a double consonant should be accentuated as in sh sh; nn' mm; g,g,; k,k; I have inserted the "i" to show the nature and quality of the sound.

There are in the Ojibway language numerous double syllables: for example, naunau or nana or nanauh; babau, baba, paupa, paupau, papau. A double syllable indicates repetition and continuation.

bimossae = he (she) walks
baumossae = he (she) walks about, strolling
babaumossae = (she) walks about, here and there, thither and yon.

I hope that this Outline will serve as a useful guide to the Ojibway language.

BJ

11

Beyer

In the Beginning

According to the tradition of the Anishinaubaeg, soil spread on the back of a giant turtle grew into an island and became their home. They called it Michillimackinac, "The Place of the Great Turtle." The first people to live there were conceived in the sky and born to Skywoman on this island.

Just how Nanabush, a Manitou, was conceived and came into being is a mystery. There are several accounts as to the manner of his coming to the people who call themselves the Anishinaubaeg.

In one story, the Manitou Ae-pungishimook came to the land of the Anishinaubaeg and fell in love with the daughter of N'okomiss, whose name was Winonah. The Manitou married Winonah and they had three sons. By the time Nanabush, their fourth son, came into being, his brothers had grown and gone from home. Even his father had deserted Winonah and returned to his own land. Shortly after Nanabush was born, his mother died.

Nanabush is an orphan, without mother or father, without brothers or sisters. he has only old N'okomiss, his grandmother, to look to for love and affection; he has only N'okomiss for guidance and knowledge and sustenance.

Nanabush learned of the world as other little Anishinaubae boys learned of it. Even though he was a Manitou with all the advantages of a being of this nature, still Nanabush had to discover and understand the world and the beings in it as one of the Anishinaubae people.

Nanabush grew up into a man with supernatural powers. He would defend the tribe from its many enemies - evil Manitous, Weendigoes, Giant Beavers, Giant Bears, Giant Moose, Giant Sturgeon, who preyed upon the people. The disturbances they caused often threatened to destroy villages and lands.

1

Nanabush Pursues the Giant Beaver

N'okomiss and Nanabush were camped at *Tahquamenon*, "the shallow bed river." This river emptied into the eastern end of a great lake not far from *Boweting*, "the place of the Rapids,", now called Sault Ste. Marie.

Here the Giant Beaver had constructed an immense dam blocking up the waters of *Ojibway-kitchi-gummeeng*, Lake Superior, then known as the Great Lake of the Ojibway. This dam caused parts of *Wisconsin*, "the land of the muskrat," to be flooded.

Nanabush erected a camp at the south end of the dam near Bay Mills, or *Ginozhaekaunning*, "the place of the pike." He installed his grandmother there to keep watch for the Giant Beaver, raising an alarm if she saw the enemy. Then he was on his way.

Nanabush pursued the Giant Beaver along the Grand Sable Dunes, known in those days as *Nigowidjiw*, "sand mountains," on the south shores of Lake Superior. On past the Painted Rocks, *Mazinaubikaung*, he hurried, until he drove the Giant Beaver into a shallow bay.

To prevent the cornered enemy from escaping, Nanabush built his own dam, extending from *Odenah*, "town", to *Oshki-odenah* or "new town," since renamed Bayfield. Then Nanabush went off, looking for the village of "Bad River," *mashki-zeebi*.

While he was gone, the Giant Beaver tore through the dam and escaped. Parts of the dam were deposited in the channel just off shore and formed the knot of islands known today as the Apostle Islands. Chequamegon Point, once known as *Zhaegawauyaumikong*, "the long narrow span," lies below them.

Up to this point Nanabush had conducted his pursuit on foot. Now he borrowed, without permission, a canoe from the people at *Moningwonaekauning*, "the place of the lapwing or plover," now La Pointe, and resumed his pursuit on water. That night he reached *Kitchi-bitobigong*, "the Great Pond place," now Grand Marais, where Nanabush camped for the night.

Rested, he continued his chase the following morning. He stopped briefly at *Kitchi-winigumeeng*, Grand Portage, to inquire whether the people had seen the Giant Beaver. "Just up ahead," they said.

Up ahead was Thunder Bay, then *Gamanautigawaeyauk*, or "the land of many river islands" where the Giant Beaver thought he could hide from Nanabush. Still, despite all the inlets, marshes, underwater caverns, deep waters, where one might lie low almost indefinitely, Nanabush flushed out the Giant Beaver.

He drove the Giant Beaver up a river into Lake Nipigon, *Animibeegong*, "along the water's edge." Again the Giant Beaver escaped, but was growing weary from having to stay submerged for long periods of time.

At *Michipicoten*, "the place of broken craggy highlands," there lived a colony of Giant Beavers in a giant village made of huge stone

lodges. Here the Giant Beaver believed he would find safety with his kin. But there was no safeguard from Nanabush's fury or his war-club. Nanabush destroyed all the lodges and beavers, vowing that Giant Beavers would never again harm the Anishinaubaeg. In so doing, he altered once and for all the character of the land. Since then it has been called Michipicoten.

The Giant beaver ought to have been clubbed along with his kind. Instead, he escaped. Despite the head start of his quarry, Nanabush overtook the Giant Beaver in a bay. Down he dove to face his enemy. Underwater they struggled and the fighting became so fierce the bay welled up as if it were boiling. Thus the battle waters became known as *Batchawana,* "the place of the welling waters."

As long as he could hold his breath, Nanabush fought the beaver. Eventually he was forced to surface for air, but if the giant beaver had had his wits about him he should have locked an iron grip on Nanabush. Instead, he was too anxious to make his escape. While Nanabush was recovering his breath on the surface, the Giant Beaver made straight for his dam back at Sault Ste. Marie.

By swimming underwater, the Giant Beaver also slipped by the watching N'okomiss and broke through the dam. Water poured through the breach, washing debris down the current into the southeastern shores of Georgian Bay and there deposited it in the form of 30,000 islands.

To deal with his grandmother's neglect of duty then would have delayed Nanabush in his pursuit. He would settle with her later.

18

Quickly but cautiously he portaged to get by the rapids, and once safe, leapt into his canoe and paddled furiously, throwing up sprays of water behind his craft.

By following the wake on the surface of the waters, it was easy to trail the Giant Beaver to the funnel of waters at *Aumidjiwunaung,* "the place where the waters collect," now known as Sarnia. Nanabush then paddled on through *Nissodjiwunaung,* or "Three Channels", now called Walpole Island.

Quickly he paddled across Lake St. Clair, *Wauwi-autinoong,* "the round lake" and then drifted out onto Lake *Erie,* "the place of the panther or cougar," according to the Tuscarora people, and *Waubishkegokitchigummeeng,* or "the white breakers," to the Anishinaubaeg.

Nanabush followed the Giant Beaver's trail to Niagara Falls. When he saw the falls and its strength, its long drop, he believed that no one, not even a Giant Beaver, could survive the plunge over "the great falls", *Kitchi-gaugeedjiwung.* For the first time, Nanabush discontinued his pursuit.

Back Nanabush went to his ancestral home.

2

Nanabush Chases the Weendigoes

Some time after his return, Nanabush received a summons from the Anishinaebaeg living on the shores of *Lake Nipissing*, ''at the place of the waters.'' Attacks were being made on their homes by the evil, man-eating Weendigoes. They needed help.

On his arrival, Nanabush went directly to the lair of the monsters at the meeting place of the Ottawa and *Matawa*, ''where the current or flow begins,'' rivers. Nanabush roared out a challenge. His call echoed through the hills and canyons. Dozens of Weendigoes charged from the lairs. Nanabush had not expected to meet more than two or three. Now, bearing down upon him were more than twenty Weendigoes of the most dreadful aspect.

Nanabush took to his heels, but the monsters were faster. Just as one reached out a hand to grab him, Nanabush said a prayer on the shore of Lake Nipissing. Rocks formed instantly from one point of land to another, creating a bridge for his escape.

Along these rocks Nanabush raced, leaping from one to another. But still the Weendigoes came on his heels, drawing closer. Nanabush prayed once more. Behind him the rocks on which the Weendigoes ran disappeared and these Weendigoes vanished into the water, never to be seen again.

3

Nanabush Tries to Lose N'okomiss

After his triumph over the Weendigoes, Nanabush fetched his grandmother before proceeding to *Couchiching,* ''at the edge of a whirlpool,'' where he pitched his camp among the people of the area.

Because moose and geese were more plentiful further to the north, it suited Nanabush's love for travel to go in search of game in the north. Despite his affection for his grandmother, there were times when he found N'okomiss to be a burden. And this trip was no different. Not only did Nanabush have to carry his grandmother during his trek from one place to another, he had to look after her in every other respect. More than anything else, N'okomiss' forgetfulness annoyed Nanabush.

Nanabush had got as far as West Bay, *Mitchigee-waedinong,* ''the bare west place,'' when his grandmother remembered that she had left her medicine bag behind at the previous camping place. By now Nanabush, who had back-tracked too often for his grandmother, had grown weary of going back. No more would he go back. He threw his grandmother into a lake, *Lake Mindemoya,* ''the old woman lake.''

Thinking he had got rid of his grandmother, Nanabush turned southward by way of the North Channel, getting as far as ''the bay of beavers" or *Wikwemikong,* on that first day. There he slew many beavers. With his canoe full of meat, Nanabush crossed to the north shore, navigating through "the narrows" known as *Zheebaunauning* at Killarney.

Like a good seaman, Nanabush hugged the north shore that sheltered him from the north and east winds until he arrived in *Shawanaga,* "the south portage," where he pitched his camp to hunt ducks.

As if the Manitous were against Nanabush, the ducks by-passed Shawanaga, and while Nanabush was awaiting the arrival of the birds he ate his entire supply of beaver meat. With nothing to eat but dried berries and with winter soon to come, Nanbush decamped. He put ashore on Parry Island, *Waussaukissing,* or "brightly reflecting", to replenish his stock of berries. To his disappointment there was nothing on the island to eat except some roots which he had to dig up with his bare hands. Not very tasty perhaps, but roots kept Nanabush alive until his return to Couchiching.

At Couchiching there was no shortage of food. In all his travels, he had never seen anyone fish the way that these Anishinaubaeg fished. They constructed fences in the water, *mitchikun,* "weir", to direct trout, whitefish, and other fish along a certain course. The area came to be known as the "district of fences", *mitchikunneeng.*

In the meantime, N'okomiss returned, having survived the waters of Lake Mindemoya. Nanabush was secretly relieved when she came back.

It was getting late in the fall when Nanabush set out to hunt meat for the winter. By now he and N'okomiss had wearied of fish and longed for meat. From Couchiching Nanabush went directly north and then angled to the east until he came to a village whose people were also of the Anishinaubae tribe. The people there welcomed Nanabush and invited him to hunt and to fish with them in Chemong Lake, the Great Loon Lake.

During the time that Nanabush camped in the Chemong area, he frequently went hunting alone. On one of these expeditions Nanabush had not killed anything and he was hungry on his return to his camp.

At dusk he came upon a solitary wigwaum set on a point of land. He could tell from the smoke rising from the fireplace that a meal was under preparation, and from the aroma that corn-meal breads were being baked. Hungry and in need of nourishment, Nanabush beached his canoe.

"I see that I'm on time. I would be very grateful if you extended some compassion to me. I've been hunting all day without seeing so much as a rabbit. Even if you gave me no more than a crust of bread, it would be quite enough to bear me home."

"You ask what don't I have to give. I have scarcely enough for myself."

"I won't complain. I'll be quite satisfied with whatever little you can spare; Kitchi-Manitou will be as kind to you as you are to me."

"This is all I have for my own meal," the old women told

Nanabush, showing him dough the size of a large potato. This the old woman broke and made into a pattie in the palm of her hands.

"This is all I can spare," the woman said.

"That will do," Nanabush answered the old woman. "I'm tired. I'll sleep while you are cooking. Wake me up when you are finished."

The old woman made no reply but went on with her business of cooking. She placed the pattie near the flames on a flat rock. Before her eyes the pattie of dough grew and grew, until it was as large as a pumpkin. As the old woman considered the bread, it was much too fine to give to a beggar and to a stranger. Accordingly, she put it away in her wigwaum, along with the other corn breads that she had baked. A second time she broke a piece from the remaining dough, except that the piece was now smaller than the first. This too swelled beyond the old women's expectations, a round of bread the size of a pumpkin. This bread too exceeded in size what the beggar had asked for. She hid it for her own use. The old woman broke off still another piece, no bigger than an acorn. It too, as by miracle, swelled in mass. Just as she had not been able to part with the other rounds of bread, the old woman could not give this last bread to the beggar, even though she now had more than enough for her own needs. She put it away with the other rounds of bread.

Nanabush woke up. "How's the bread that you were going to bake for me coming along? It must be done by now."

"It's such a shame," the old woman explained, "but I had a dreadful accident while I was cooking. The bread that I was baking for you

fell into the fire.....it burned to cinders. I'm sorry, I have nothing else to offer you."

Instantly, Nanabush flared into anger.

"You aren't telling the truth. You are so stingy that you hid the bread from me. You care nothing for others; you care only for yourself. All right! No more! For holding back food from me, you will spend the rest of your days as a bird. You will eat nothing but worms, which you will extract from trees, one at a time. You will be a woodpecker. And the trees themselves will hold back food from you just as you withheld food from your fellow human being."

How long did Nanabush stay in this part of what is now *Ontario* "a fine lake"? Generations; perhaps even longer. It was hard for the people to let Nanabush return to his ancestral home. Only a few, only the very old, remember his presence.

4

Nanabush's Bad Habits Spoil His Hunting

Even before he left, couriers from the Menominee, the Wild Rice people, cousins of the Anishinaubaeg, came to Nanabush with offerings of tobacco. He was asked to abide with them for a while and be a patron to the tribe. Nanabush broke camp at once and, taking his grandmother, accompanied the Menominee messengers.

It was for the purpose of tutoring young men in the art of hunting that the Menominee invited Nanabush, whom they called Winabozho, to live with them. They had heard that Nanabush was a skilled hunter. During the first few months he lived with the Menominee, Nanabush did little else but lead hunting expeditions. Even though his skill was renowned, Nanabush would have been a better hunter had he been more diligent and hard working. But Nanabush was on the lazy side, and distrusting.

He was at the south end of Lake Michigan, *mishi-gummeeng*, ''great body of water.'' After two days of fruitless hunting, Nanabush began to question the traditional techniques of stalking game. Giving the matter a great deal of thought, he reckoned that there had to be a better way of hunting; one that required far less effort. He decided there was hardly a more potent weapon than the smell possessed by the skunk. If its force and range were increased, the skunk charge could be used to bring down deer, moose and ducks with great ease.

Nanabush went to the Giant Skunk with the idea of converting the skunk repellent into a hunting instrument. The request seemed reasonable to the Giant Skunk, so a few adjustments were made to Nanabush's body, providing him with a lustier charge than ordinary skunks. One whiff would fell a victim without killing him. As the Giant Skunk explained the manner of use, he warned Nanabush not to waste a single charge. Otherwise he would lose the talent completely.

On the way to the hunting grounds, Nanabush's doubts began to nag him. Just to make sure, Nanabush fired a test charge at some plants which promptly drooped down, overcome by the fumes. Nanabush himself was stricken. To this day, the place is known as Chicago, from *Zhigaug,* either "the place of the skunk" or "the wild leek."

Further up the coast at Milwaukee, *mino-aki,* meaning "the fair, fertile land," Nanabush came upon a deer. He fired a charge from the skunk position as he had been instructed to do, but nothing happened. The deer did not fall down as expected. Nanabush had wasted a charge on the plants.

In looking after the Menominee, Nanabush lived the life of a nomad, going from village to village. He often accompanied bands of people in their migrations or in their wild rice gathering expeditions in the autumn, north of Lake Shawano, *zhauwun* or "south," and elsewhere. On a few occasions Nanabush and his companions ventured into the land of the Winnebago to fish on Lake Winnebago, *Weenipeego,* or ''lake of murky waters.''

In memory of Winabozho, as the Menominee called Nanabush, they told and re-told stories of the deeds that he performed on their behalf. Of the accidents that he suffered as a result of his impulsiveness, his tendency toward laziness and his inability to follow instructions, they said nothing.

5

Nanabush Challenges a Weendigo

Nanabush's northwest brothers and sisters now required his companionship and guardianship. It was time to move on. To console his Menominee kinsmen on his leaving, Nanabush promised to return to them frequently.

It was a long and dangerous undertaking to cross the rugged lands inhabited only by Weendigoes and other unnamed monsters. Nanabush risked the journey alone, leaving his grandmother in the care of neighbours during his absence.

The course took Nanabush to the very edge of the plains. At that time there were no Anishinaubaeg living on the plains. Nanabush came to Cloquet, *Pashkoninitigong,* ''the barren place.'' Here the people pleaded with Nanabush to hunt down and kill a Weendigo who had been wreaking havoc with their lives.

Nanabush was outraged by their reports of the evil of the Weendigo. He seized his war-club and performed the dance of war, reciting past exploits. As he acted out his previous triumphs, Nanabush described how he had overcome his other opponents as a token of what he intended to do to the Weendigo. Nanabush was like that: impulsive and anxious to avenge the downtrodden.

Nanabush set out brimming with vengeance and confidence.

The trail led Nanabush down the upper reaches of the Mississippi River, or *Mishiseepi,* "the great river," to Mille Lacs, *Mishi-sagaigun,* "the big lake" in Minnesota, where the Weendigo was camping.

Nanabush went directly to the enemy and challenged him to battle. The Weendigo stood up to accept the challenge. He was six times the stature of an ordinary man. Nanabush turned on both heels.

Ahead, somewhere in the distance and beyond the horizon, was cover, where he could hide if he could outrun the Weendigo. Nanabush ran with dread. Behind, and within hearing, was the Weendigo, relentless in his pursuit. Nanabush ran, perspiration streaming down his chest and back. He ran until he came to a lake. Here he launched a canoe that he found beached.

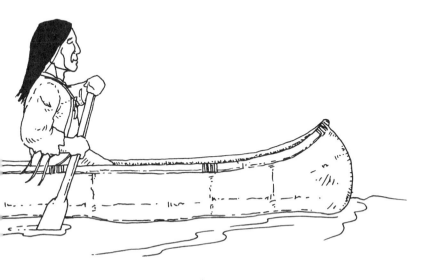

Nanabush managed to cross Leech Lake, *Ga-sagaskwadjimekag*, "the place where leeches abound," in the borrowed canoe. But he managed merely to delay the inevitable. At *Nay-Tauh-waush*, "remarkable flyer," in the White Earth region, *Gawababiganikag* or "white clay," the Weendigo caught Nanabush.

As a cat toys with a mouse before the kill, so did the Weendigo toy with Nanabush. Nanabush was forced to collect an enormous pile of firewood and construct a roasting spit. Weeping and crying for mercy, Nanabush prepared his own funeral pyre.

Although every creature and being in Gawababiganikag country heard him, it was the bold weasel who came to Nanabush's aid. The weasel told Nanabush he must weep more softly and to beg for mercy and for his life. Seldom had Nanabush done what he was told, but on this occasion he did.

To the Weendigo the words and the tone of the weeping were like a soothing lullaby. He fell asleep. Once the Weendigo was asleep, Nanabush ran the Weendigo through with a stake rendered even more deadly because it was tempered in fire.

6

Nanabush Flies with the Geese

After his escape, Nanabush spent some months at Ponemah, *Boonimau,* ''he/she stops talking to him/her'' or ''later,'' in the district of Red Lake, *Miskwagamiwi-sagaigun,* ''red watered lake.'' Only by stealing away one night did Nanabush manage to leave for Net Lake, *Suppeewigo sagaigun.*

Nanabush at last came to a land that was very different from what he had been accustomed to. Its people had not yet given it a name. The land was one mighty prairie, *mishkodae,* ''without hills or forests,'' inhabited by animals and birds he had never seen. For all its endlessness and changelessness, the plain was bountiful and its animals, rich in fat and flesh, were beyond counting.

The people were harvesting wild rice for the coming winter when large flocks of geese descended upon this unnamed lake to feed and rest for a while before resuming their migration. Learning that they were bound for the land of perpetual summer to escape the winter, Nanabush received permission to accompany the geese. In order to fly, the chief of all the geese gave Nanabush a pair of wings, a rudder and then feathered him. The main rule in flight is not to look down, warned the chief goose before take-off.

When the flock lifted into the sky, likewise did Nanabush, as if he had been so doing all his life.

There was gloom in the Anishinaubae lodges and villages the entire winter. The people longed for the return of Nanabush.

Never had they looked for the coming of spring more anxiously than they now did. Long before the geese were due to arrive, crowds of Anishinaubaeg gathered on the shores of the lake to welcome Nanabush and celebrate his return with a festival.

Nanabush was in the first flock that appeared in the southern sky and the people, recognizing him, sent up a mighty cheer of welcome. When he heard the acclaim, Nanabush was moved by the affection of his brothers and sisters and he looked down.

At that moment he fell to the earth, legs and arms flailing, feathers fluttering in the air as they were stripped from his wings and rudder. Nanabush plunged into the shallow waters of the lake and was imbedded in the mud. After rescuing Nanabush, the Anishinaubaeg cleansed him of the muck, but in washing Nanabush, the waters of the lake were forever begrimed. From that day the Anishinaubaeg called it *Weenipeegosheeng*, ''the murky watered lake,'' or Winnipeg.

7

Nanabush Finds Strange Dance Partners

It is said that Nanabush crossed the Great Plains, scaled the mountains, trekked the tundra and even went southward far enough to leave a name to a valley that appealed to him. He called it simply *Pusudinauh,* "a valley," that is now known as Pasadena, a long way down in southern California.

But of all the lands that he saw, Nanabush preferred lands with lakes and rivers, valleys and highlands. He was as fond of moose and deer and partridge as he was of trout and whitefish. Always he came back to the land of lakes and rivers.

Whenever Nanabush tired of buffalo meat during his stay in *Manitoba,* the "abode of the manitou between two lakes," he headed east. He would pitch camp with the Anishinaubaeg of *Keewatin,* "the north wind place," with whom he would hunt and fish in the countless bays and shoals in the area.

Despite his love of people, Nanabush never had a lasting friendship or a permanent home. Home was where he pitched his tent; home was the land of lakes and rivers, highlands and lowlands, endless forests and numerous glades. Wherever he went Nanabush was always welcome to stay for as long as it pleased him.

The People at *Sabaskong,* "the passage way," were as generous a people as any and ever willing to share their fire. They invited Nanabush to spend his winter with them. With game plentiful and company warm, Nanabush would not hunger nor would he be lonely.

For Nanabush, it was one of the best winters he had known. He had ample food.

One spring night, the Anishinaubaeg were awakened by the throb of a drum, the echo of a chant, and the break of water. Alarmed, they went down to the shore to see who was making a festival. In the dark they could just discern the figure of Nanabush high stepping and dancing in the marsh water amongst tall bulrushes. But his chant was clear:

> I will drum as long as you,
> I will chant as long as you,
> I will dance as long as you.
> Longer will I drum.
> Longer will I chant.
> Longer will I dance.

At dawn Nanabush discovered that he had been dancing with bulrushes. For days afterward the Anishinaubaeg teased Nanabush, "Make sure you know who you are dancing with next time."

Throughout it all Nanabush retained his good humour, sometimes explaining that he was practising an old dance or that he was creating a new dance.

8

Nanabush Nearly Drowns

"Don't stay away too long," the Anishinaubaeg at Sabaskong reminded Nanabush as he prepared to move back to Couchiching in northwest Ontario. On his arrival, the Couchiching Anishinaubaeg welcomed Nanabush with a feast, as if he were coming home.

Though he could perform marvellous deeds as a spirit, Nanabush as a human being could commit the most stupid of blunders. He knew matters that men did not know and was ignorant of some of the most basic of human knowledge. Besides, he lacked a certain degree of common sense. Otherwise, he would not have suffered the accident that not only broke his nose, but led to his near drowning. It came about in the following manner.

The Anishinaubaeg took Nanabush on their berry picking expedition. Instead of following the others who knew their way, Nanabush took the lead. He saw the reflection of overhanging berries on a pool of water. Wanting nothing more than to be the first, Nanabush dove into the shallows. His followers laughed. And they laughed until they realized Nanabush had failed to surface.

Someone waded into the shallows. Had it not been for the presence of his companions who pulled him out of the water, Nanabush might have drowned. Still, for all his blundering, the Anishinaubaeg thought no less of Nanabush.

9

Nanabush Learns the Ways of the North

From Couchiching, Nanabush wound his way northward, camping at *Pikangikum,* ''the lake of calm waters,'' and at *Wunnumin,* ''the lake of beaver meal fragments,'' before going on to Kasabonika, or *Kaussaubonikauk,* ''the narrow place,'' *Weagamow,* ''Round Lake''ʹ and finally on to *Kitchi-numae-gooss zaugigun,*''Big Trout Lake ''.

The Anishinaubaeg here were rugged, as rugged as the land, but as generous as any Anishinaubaeg anywhere.

Though Nanabush learned the ways of the north, obeyed the customs and the traditions of his northern brothers and sisters, he could not change or modify his character.

Just south of Kitchi-numaegooss zaugigun Nanabush killed an enormous moose. By custom he ought to have offered a portion to the jays who had conducted him to the game. Nanabush did not do so because he feared he would have less for himself were he to sacrifice even the innards to worthless birds who had not contributed an ounce of energy to his success. Better that he have all for himself.

As he regarded his moose, Nanabush was at a loss as to where to start in butchering the beast. He didn't want his brothers and sisters of the north to regard him as backward in the matter of ritual.

While he pondered the northern practice for quartering moose, Nanabush fell asleep. When he awakened later, he found only the skull. Wolves had made off with the choicest portions.

Nanabush was desperately hungry. With the aid of a giant mouse, he himself was transformed into a mouse, and as such burrowed his way into the skull to nibble on what little meat remained inside. His violent movements in tearing strips of meat caused the skull to tilt and roll down the slope into a lake.

It was only by churning his hindquarters that Nanabush could keep the skull afloat. From the distance, the floating skull looked like a live moose to the hunters standing on shore. Quickly they boarded their canoes and when they were near enough, cracked the skull open with their clubs. They never saw the tiny mouse swim away, and thus Nanabush escaped with his life again.

Later one old hunter offered him some advice. "When you're quartering moose, it doesn't matter whether you start with the left or the right hindquarter."

Once Nanabush learned how to hunt and adopted the ways of the north, he lived a good life. Fact was, he forgot his ancestral home for a long time. Many years later he remembered his grandmother and his home. In recalling N'okomiss, Nanabush grew lonesome and he bade farewell to his brothers and sisters of Kitchi-numaegooss zaugigunning to return to Tahquamenon in northern Michigan. Again Nanabush was on the road travelling to a far away town, only this time it was home.

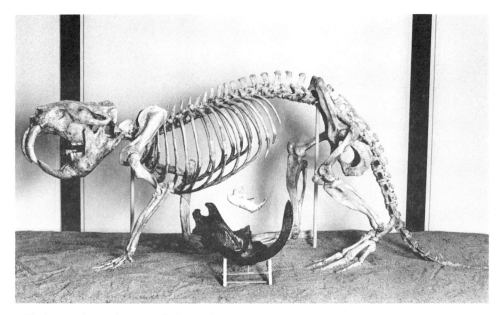

Skeleton of giant beaver - below it the lower jaws of the modern beaver (white) and of the giant beaver (black).

From The Science Museum, (St. Paul, Minnesota).

Courtesy the National Museum of Natural Sciences, Ottawa, Canada.

Editor's Note

Many of the myths and fables of all cultures often stem from some ancient truth. Just so, many of our Native People's legends handed down from the elders, originated from an actual fact or happening. They are a mix of the real and the fanciful.

The modern beaver did indeed have a giant ancestor. Scientists have discovered evidence that it existed three to five million years ago in North America and Eurasia. It may have weighed six or seven times as much as the modern beaver, and was over twice as long. Fossils have been found in the area south of the Great Lakes as well as in the Old Crow region of the Yukon Territory. Three almost complete specimens have been found in Indiana and Minnesota.

Near New Noxville, Ohio, paleontologists (experts on ancient life) discovered what they think was possibly a giant beaver lodge. It was thought to have been around 1.2 m high and 2.4 m wide

These ice-age creatures lacked the modern beaver's flat, broad tail. Theirs was rounder like a muskrat's thus the many Native legends telling "how the beaver got its tail." The giant beaver's cutting teeth were up to 15 cm long, giving them a truly ferocious appearance.

Perhaps the giant could not build dams like those of the modern beaver and was not able to travel as easily over dry land. As the land began to dry up, there were fewer swamps bordering lakes and ponds. Not being able to move readily on to new swamps, and competition with modern beavers may have led to the giant beaver's extinction.

They did live at the time of the early people of North America and thus the tales of it being pursed by the Manitou, Nanabush, sprang from the experiences of this country's first people.